THE SCIENCE OF RELIGION

THE SCIENCE OF RELIGION

SWAMI YOGANANDA

GYAN

Published by

Gyan Publishing House
5, Ansari Road
Daryaganj, New Delhi-110002
Phone: 011-47034999, 9811692060
E-mail: books@gyanbooks.com

Distribution Network
gyanbooks.com
India, USA, Canada, UK, Australia

ISBN: 978-93-7097-671-9 (HB)

First Published, 1925

2nd Impression 2025

Printed at: Gyan Press, Delhi.

THE SCIENCE OF RELIGION
Author: SWAMI YOGANANDA

SWAMI YOGANANDA

THE SCIENCE OF RELIGION

BY

SWAMI YOGANANDA, A.B.

Founder of
Mt. Washington Educational Center, Los Angeles
Ranchi and Puri Brahmacharya Residential Schools in India
Sat-Sanga (Fellowship with Truth), Boston
Sat-Sanga Summer School, Waltham
Vice-President: Sadhu Sabha, India
Delegate from India to International Congress of Religions
Boston, 1920

SWAMI DHIRANANDA, M.A., Associate

FOURTH EDITION

PUBLISHED BY

YOGODA AND SAT SANGA HEADQUARTERS

MT. WASHINGTON, SAN RAFAEL AND ELYRIA STS.

LOS ANGELES, CALIF.

MCMXXV

FOR

His piety, open-handed generosity towards every worth-while movement, unbounded devotion to the cause of general education, and exclusive and pioneer patronage in the establishment of a unique residential Brahmacharya School in India

THIS BOOK IS INSCRIBED TO

THE HON'BLE MAHARAJA SIR MANINDRA CHANDRA NUNDY, K.C.I.E., OF KASIMBAZAR (BENGAL), INDIA

MEMBER, COUNCIL OF STATE, INDIA GOVERNMENT

NOTE

The first edition of this book was published in India. The second and subsequent editions, revised and enlarged, have been published in the U. S. A.

My thanks are due to Swami Dhirananda, M.A., Swami Satyananda, B.A., and Sj. Tulsinarayan Bose, for various forms of help I have received from them.

SWAMI YOGANANDA.

CONTENTS

PREFACE . . . . vii—xv

CHAPTER I . . . . 1—58

The Universality, Necessity and Oneness of Religion: Distinction between Pain, Pleasure, and Bliss: God.

CHAPTER II . . . . 59—89

The Four Fundamental Religious Methods.

CHAPTER III . . . . 90—107

The Instruments of Knowledge: The Religious Point of View.

PREFACE

This book is intended to give, in bare outline, what we should understand by religion, in order to make it universally and pragmatically necessary. It also seeks to present that aspect of the idea of the God-head which has a direct bearing on the motives and actions of every minute of our lives. It is true that God is Infinite in His nature and aspect, and it is also true that to prepare a chart detailing, so far as is consistent with reason, what God is like is only an evidence of the limitations of the human mind in its attempt to fathom God. Still it is equally true that the human mind, in spite of all its drawbacks, can not rest perfectly satisfied with what is finite. It has a natural urge to interpret what is human and finite in the light of what is super-human and infinite,— what it feels but can not express, what within it lies implicit but under circumstances refuses to be explicit.

Our ordinary conception of God is that He is Super-human, Infinite, Omnipresent, Omniscient, and the like. In this general conception there are many variations. Some call God Personal, some Impersonal, and so forth. The point emphasized in this book is that whatever conception we have of God, if it does not influence our daily conduct, if every-day life does not find an inspiration from it, and if it is not found universally necessary, then that conception is worse than useless. If God is not conceived in such a way that we can not do without Him in the satisfaction of a want, in our dealings with people, in earning money, in reading a book, in passing an examination, in the doing of the most trifling or the highest duties, then it is better we should act discreetly, taking His useless name less into churches and temples. God may be Infinite, Omnipresent, Omniscient,

Personal, Merciful, or anything, but these conceptions are not sufficiently compelling to make us try to know God. We may as well do without Him. He may be Infinite, Omnipresent, and so forth, but we have no immediate and practical use for those conceptions in our busy, rushing lives. We fall back on those conceptions only when we seek to justify, in philosophical and poetical writings, in art or in warmed-up, idealistic talks, the finite craving for something beyond; when we, with all our vaunted knowledge, are at a loss to explain some of the most common phenomena of the universe; or when we get stranded in the vicissitudes of the world. "We pray to the Ever-Merciful when we get stuck," as the Eastern maxim has it. Except for all this, we seem to get along all right in our work-a-day world without Him. These conceptions appear to be the safety-valves of our pent-up human thought. They explain Him, but do not make us seek Him. They lack motive power. We are not necessarily seeking God when we call Him Infinite, Omnipresent, All-Merciful, and so forth. These conceptions satisfy our intellect, but do not soothe our soul. If respected and cherished at heart, they may broaden us to a certain extent—may make us moral and resigned towards Him. But they do not make God our own—they are not intimate enough. They place Him aloof from everyday concern of the world. These conceptions savor of outlandishness when we are on the street, in a factory, behind a counter, or in an office. Not because we are really dead to God and religion, but because we lack a proper conception of them—a conception that can be interwoven with the fabric of daily life. What we conceive of God should be of daily, nay hourly, guidance to us. The very conception of God should stir us to seek Him in the midst of our daily lives. This is what we mean by a pragmatic and compelling conception of

God. We should take religion and God out of the sphere of belief into that of daily life. If we do not emphasize the necessity of God in every aspect of our lives and the need of religion in every minute of our existence, then God and religion drop out of our intimate daily consideration and become only a one-day-in-a-week affair. In the first chapter of this work the attempt has been made to show that *in order to understand the real necessity of God and religion we must throw emphasis on that conception of both which is most relevant to the chief aim of our daily and hourly actions.*

This book has also attempted to show the universality and unity of Religion. There have been different religions at different ages. There have been heated controversy, long warfare, and much bloodshed over them. One religion stood against another, one sect fought with another. Not only is there a variety in religions, but there is also a wide diversity of sects and opinions within the same religion.

But the question arises, when there is one God, why there should be so many religions? It may be argued that particular stages of intellectual growth and special types of mentality belonging to certain nations, due to different geographical locations and other extraneous circumstances, determine the origin of different religions, such as Hinduism and Buddhism, for the Indians and the Asia tics, Mohammedanism for the Arabs (at least at its beginning,) Christianity for the Westerners, and so forth. If by Religion we understand only practices, particular tenets, dogmas, customs and conventions, then there may be ground for the existence of so many religions; but if Religion means, primarily, God-consciousness, or the realization of God both within and without, which it really does; secondarily, a body of beliefs, tenets, and dogmas, then, strictly speaking, there is but one Religion in the world, for there is but one God; and different customs, forms of worship, tenets, and conventions may be held to form the grounds for the origin of different denominations and sects included under that one Religion. If Religion is understood in this way, then and then only can its universality be maintained, for we can not possibly universalize particular customs or conventions. Only the element common to all the so-called religions can be universalized. We can ask every one to follow that. Then can it be truly said that Religion is not only necessary but it is universal, as well. Everyone must follow the same religion, for there is but one, its universal element being one and the same. Only its customs and conventions differ.

I have tried to show in this book that *as God is one, necessary for all of us, so Religion is one, necessary and universal.* Only the roads to it may differ in some respects at the beginning. As a matter of fact, it is ludicrous to say that there are two religions, when there is but one God. There may be two denominations or sects, but there is only one Religion. What we now call different religions should be known as different denominations or sects under that one universal Religion. And what we now know as different denominations or sects should be specified as different branch cults or creeds. If we once know the meaning of the word "Religion," which we are going to discuss by and by, we shall naturally be very circumspect in the use of it. It is only the limited human point of view that overlooks the underlying universal element in the so-called different religions of the world, and this overlooking has been the cause of many evils.

This book gives a psychological definition of Religion, not an objective definition based on dogmas or tenets. In other words, it seeks to make Religion a question of our whole inward being and attitude, and not a mere observance of certains rules and precepts, nor an intellectual aquiescence, either, in certain beliefs about God, the universe, and so forth. On this psychological ground its universality has been established. I have also discussed the merits and demerits of the different methods required to be followed for the attainment of that religious consciousness which is here set forth.

In conclusion it should be remembered that when the theory and practice of Religion are poles apart, we must not stop at the theory and lose energy over comment or criticism thereon, leaving out of sight the practical aspect of it that alone can lead to its true understanding. The verification of a theory lies in practice. If a practice truly followed is found at last to militate against the theory, then, and not till then, may the theory be safely rejected.

THE SCIENCE OF RELIGION

CHAPTER I

The Universality, Necessity, and Oneness of Religion: The Distinction between Pleasure, Pain, and Bliss: God

First we must know what Religion is, then only can we judge whether it is necessary for all of us to be religious.

Without necessity there is no action. Every action of ours has an end of its own for which we perform it. People of the world act variously to accomplish various ends. There is a multiplicity of ends determining the actions of men in the world.

But is there any common and universal end of all the actions of all the people of the world? Is there *any common, highest necessity* for all of us which prompts us to all actions? A little analysis of the motives and ends of men's actions in the world shows that, though there are a thousand and one proximate or immediate ends of men in regard to the particular calling or profession which they take up, the ultimate end which all other ends merely subserve comes to be the avoidance of pain and want and the attainment of permanent Bliss. Whether we can at all permanently avoid pain and want and get Bliss is a separate question, but as a matter of fact, in all our actions, we obviously try to avoid the former and get the latter. Why does a man act as a probationer? Because he wishes to become an expert in a certain business. Why does he engage in that particular business? Because money can be earned therein. Why should money be earned at all? Because it will put an end to personal and family wants. Why must wants be fulfilled? Because pain will thereby be removed and Bliss or happiness be gained. As a matter of fact, happiness and Bliss are not the same thing. We all aim at Bliss, but through a great blunder we imagine pleasure and happiness to be Bliss. How that has come to be so will be shown presently. The ultimate motive is really Bliss, which we feel inwardly; but happiness—or pleasure—has taken its place, through our great blunder, and the latter has come to be regarded as the ultimate motive. That this is a perversion will later be obvious, though for convenience these terms may sometimes be here used interchangeably.

Thus we see that the fulfillment of some want, removal of some pain, physical or mental, from the slightest to the acutest, and the attainment of Bliss, form our ultimate end. We can not question further why Bliss is to be gained, for no answer can be given. That is our ultimate end, no matter what we do—enter a business, earn money, seek friends, write books, acquire knowledge, rule kingdoms, donate millions, explore countries, look for fame, help the needy, become philanthropists, or embrace martyrdom. And it will be shown that the seeking of God becomes a real fact to us when that end is kept rigorously in view. Millions may be the steps, myriads may be the intermediate acts and motives; but the ultimate motive is always the same—to attain permanent Bliss, even though it be through a long chain of actions. Man likes to and has to go along the chain to get to the final end. He commits suicide to end some pain, perpetrates murder to get rid of some form of want or pain or some cruel heart-thrust. He thinks he will thereby attain a real satisfaction or relief, which he mistakes for Bliss. But the point to notice is that here, too, is the same working (though wrongly) towards the ultimate end.

Some one may say, "I do not care anything about pleasure or happiness; I live life to accomplish something, to achieve success." Another says: "I want to do good in the world. I do not care whether I am in pain or not." But if you look into the minds of these people also, you will find that there is the same working towards the goal of happiness. Does the first want a success that has in its achievement no pleasure or happiness? Does the second want to do good to others, yet himself get no happiness in doing it? Obviously not. They may not mind a thousand and one physical pains or mental sufferings inflicted by others or arising out of situations incidental to the pursuit of success or the doing of good to others; but because the one finds great satisfaction in success, and the other intensely enjoys the happiness of doing good to others the former seeks success, and the latter others' good, in spite of minor troubles.

Even the most altruistic motive, the sincerest intention of advancing the good of humanity for its own sake, have sprung from the basic urge for a chastened personal happiness, approaching Bliss. But it is not the happiness of a narrow self-seeker. It is the happiness of a broad seeker of that "pure self" that is in you and me and all. This happiness is Bliss, a little alloyed. So with Pure Bliss as a personal motive for altruistic action, the altruist is not laying himself open to the charge of narrow selfishness, for one can not himself have Pure Bliss unless he is broad enough to wish and seek it for others, too. That is the world law.

So if the motives for the actions of all men are traced further and further back, the ultimate motive will be found to be the same with all—the removal of pain and the attainment of Bliss. This end being universal, it must be looked upon as the most necessary one. And what is universal and most necessary for man is, of course, religion to him. *Hence religion necessarily consists in the permanent removal of pain and the realization of Bliss or God.* And the actions which we must adopt for the permanent avoidance of pain and the realization of Bliss or God are called religious. If we understand religion in this way, then its universality becomes obvious. For no one can deny that he wants to avoid pain permanently and attain permanent Bliss. This must be universally admitted, since none can gainsay its truth. Man's very existence is bound up with it. If he says he does not want Religion, he must needs say he does not like existence, which he can not possibly do. For existence means struggle, which in ultimate analysis means satisfying of wants, that one may attain Bliss. And this is what we understand by Religion.

You want to live because you love Religion. Even if you committed suicide it would be because you love Religion, too; for by doing that you think you will attain a happier state than you find while living. At any rate, you think you will be rid of some pain that is bothering you. In this case your religion is crude—too crude to bear the name of religion. But it is Religion, just the same. Your goal is perfectly right, the same that all persons have. For both you and they want to get happiness, or Bliss. But your means are ridiculous. Because of your ignorance you do not know what will bring you to Bliss, the goal of happiness; so you think of killing yourself to get it.

So in one sense every one in the world is religious, inasmuch as every one is trying to get rid of want and pain, and gain Bliss. Every one is working for the same goal. But in a strict sense only a few in the world are religious, for only a few in the world, though they have the same goal as all others, know the most effective means for removing, for good, all pain or want—physical, mental, or spiritual—and gaining permanent Bliss.

You have to bid good-bye for a while to the rigidly narrow orthodox conception of Religion, though that conception is in a remote way connected with the conception I am bringing out. If for some time you do not go to church or temple, or attend some of its ceremonies or forms, meantime working toward religion in your daily life by being calm, poised, concentrated, charitable, squeezing happiness from the most trying situations, then ordinary people of a pronounced orthodox or narrow bent will nod their heads and declare that, though you are trying to be good, still, from the point of view of real religion, or in the eyes of God, you are "falling off," as you did not of late enter the precinct of the holy places. While of course there can not be any valid excuse for permanently keeping away from the holy places, there can not, on the other hand, be any legitimate reason for one's being considered more religious for attending church, while at the same time neglecting to apply in daily life the principles which the church upholds, viz., those that make ultimately for the attainment of permanent Bliss. Religion is not dove-tailed with the pews of the church, nor is it bound up with the ceremonies performed therein. If you have an attitude of reverence, if you live your daily life always with a view to how you may bring undisturbed Bliss-consciousness into it, you will be just as religious out of the church as in it. Of course this should not be understood as an argument for forsaking the church, for the church is usually a real help in many ways. The point is that you should put forth just as much effort outside of the church hours to gain eternal happiness as you forego while from the pews you are passively enjoying a good sermon. Not that listening is not a good thing, in its way, for it certainly is.

The word religion is derived from the Latin *religare*, to bind (see p. 58). What binds, whom does it bind, and why? Leaving aside any orthodox explanation, it stands to reason that it is "we" who are bound. What binds us? Not chains or shackles, of course. We are talking of Religion, not of a slave dealer, so can not be bound that way. Religion may be said to bind us by rules, laws, or injunctions only. And why? To make us slaves? To disallow us the birthright of free thinking or free action? That is unreasonable. Religion must have a sufficient motive, its motive in "binding" us must also be good. The very fact of binding, then, is not enough; there must be a purpose or motive for binding us, which is the chief thing. What is that motive? The only rational answer we can give is that Religion binds us by rules, laws, injunctions, in order that we may not degenerate, that we may not have pain, misery, suffering—bodily, mentally, or Spiritually. (Bodily and mental suffering we know. But what is Spiritual suffering? To be in ignorance of the Spirit is Spiritual suffering. The latter is present, always, though often unnoticed, in every limited creature, while bodily and mental suffering come and go.) What other motive of the word "binding" than the above can we ascribe to religion that is not either nonsensical or repelling? Obviously other motives, if any, must be subservient to the one given.

Is not the definition already given of Religion consistent with the above-mentioned motive of the word "binding," the root meaning of Religion? We said that Religion, in part, consists in the permanent avoidance of pain, misery, suffering. Now Religion can not lie merely in getting rid of something, such as pain, but it must also lie in getting hold of something else. It can not be purely negative, but must be positive, too. How can we permanently get away from pain without holding to its opposite — Bliss? Though Bliss is not exactly opposite to pain, it is, at any rate, a positive consciousness to which we can cling in order to get away from pain. We can not, of course, forever hang in the air of a neutral feeling—that is neither pain nor the reverse. I repeat that Religion consists not only in the avoidance of pain, suffering, etc., but also in the attainment of Bliss, or God (that Bliss and God in one sense mean the same thing will be discussed later).

By looking, then, into the motive of the root meaning of Religion ("binding") we arrive at the same definition of Religion as we reached by the analysis of man's motive for action.

Religion is a question of fundamentals. If our fundamental motive is the seeking of Bliss, or happiness, if there is not a single act we do, not a single moment we live, that is not determined ultimately by that final motive, should we not call this craving a deep-seated one in human nature? And what can Religion be if it is not somehow intertwined with the deep-rooted craving of human nature? Religion, if it is to be anything that has life value, must base itself on a life instinct or craving. This is an *a priori* plea for the conception of Religion set forth in this book.

If you say there are many other human instincts (social, self-preserving, etc.) besides a craving for happiness, and ask why we should not interpret Religion in the light of those instincts, too, the answer is that those instincts are either subservient to the instinct of seeking happiness or are too indissolubly connected with the latter to affect substantially our interpretation of Religion.

To revert once more to the former argument (page 6), that which is universal and most necessary to man is Religion to him. If what is most necessary and universal is not Religion to him, what then can it be? That which is most accidental and variable can not be it, of course. If we try to make money the one and only thing requiring attention in our life, then money becomes Religion to us—"the Dollar is our God." The predominant life motive, whatever it may be, is Religion to us. Leave aside here the orthodox interpretation, for principles of action, and not intellectual profession of dogmas, or observance of ceremonies, determine, without the need of our personal advertisement, what religion we have. We need not wait for either the theologian or the minister to name our sect or

Religion for us—our principles and actions have a million tongues to tell it to us and others. But the amusing part of it all is that back of whatsoever thing we worship with blind exclusiveness is always one fundamental motive. That is, if we make money, business, or obtaining the necessities or luxuries of life the be-all and end-all of our existence, still back of our action lies a deeper motive: we seek these things because they banish pain and bring happiness. This fundamental motive is humanity's real Religion; other secondary motives form pseudo-religions. Because Religion is not conceived in a universal way it is relegated to the region of clouds, or thought to be a fashionable diversion for women, the aged, or the feeble.

Thus we see that the Universal Religion (or Religion conceived in this universal way) is practically or *pragmatically* necessary. Its necessity is not artificial or forced. Though in the heart its necessity is perceived, yet unfortunately we are not always fully alive to it. Had we been so, pain would long since have disappeared from the world. For ordinarily what a man thinks to be really necessary he will seek at all hazards. If the earning of money is thought by a man to be really necessary for the support of his family, he will not shrink from running into dangers to secure it. It is a pity we do not consider Religion to be necessary in the same way. Instead, we regard it as an ornament, a decoration, and not a component part of man's life.

It is also a great pity that though the aim of every man in this world is necessarily religious, inasmuch as he is working always to remove want and attain Eternal Bliss, yet due to certain grave errors he has been misdirected and led to consider the true Religion, the definition of which we have just given, as a thing of minor importance. What is the cause of this? Why do we not perceive its real necessity in place of its apparent necessity? The answer is—*society*, and our inherent tendencies in an indirect way. It is the company we keep that determines for us the necessity we feel for different things. To do good to people is what has been taught from our childhood as necessary and edifying, and so we now believe it. Consider the influence of persons and circumstances. If you wish to orientalize an occidental, place him in the midst of the Asiatics; or if you want to occidentalize an oriental, plant him among Europeans—and mark the results. It is obvious—inevitable. The man of the West learns to love the customs, habits, dress, modes of living and thought and manner of viewing things of the East, and the man of the East comes to like those of the West. The very standard of truth seems to them to vary. However, most people will agree that the worldly life, with its cares and pleasures, weal and woe, is worth living.

But of the *necessity of the Universal Religion few or none* will ever remind us, and so we are not quite alive to it. It is a truism that man can not look beyond the circle in which he is placed. Whatever falls within his own circle he justifies, follows, imitates, emulates, and feels to be the standard of thought and conduct. What is beyond his own sphere he overlooks or lessens the importance of. A lawyer will praise and be most attentive to what concerns law. Other things will, as a rule, have less importance for him.

The pragmatical or practical necessity of the Universal Religion is often understood as merely a theoretical necessity, Religion being considered an object of intellectual concern. If we know the religious ideal merely through our intellect, we think we have reached this ideal and that it is not required to live it or realize it. It is a great mistake on our part to confuse pragmatical necessity with theoretical necessity. Many would perhaps admit, on a little reflection, that Universal Religion is surely the permanent avoidance of pain and the conscious realization of Bliss, *but few, due to their inertness, understand the importance and practical necessity that this religion carries with it.*

* * * * *

Now it is necessary for us to investigate the ultimate cause of pain and suffering, mental and physical, in the avoidance of which the Universal Religion partly consists.

First of all we should assert, from our common universal experience, that we are always conscious of ourselves as the active power performing all of our mental and bodily acts. Many different functions are we performing, indeed—perceiving, apperceiving, thinking, remembering, feeling, acting, etc. Yet underlying these functions we can perceive that there is an "Ego," or "Self," which governs them and thinks of itself as substantially the same through all its past and present existence. The Bible says, "Know ye not that ye are Gods and that the Spirit of God dwelleth in thee?" All of us as individuals are so many reflected spiritual selves of the universal *Blissful Spirit—God.* Just as there appear many images of the one sun, when reflected in a number of vessels full of water, so are we apparently divided into many souls, occupying this bodily and mental vehicle, and thus outwardly separated from the One Universal Spirit. In reality, God and man are one, and this separation is only apparent.

Now, being blessed and reflected *Spiritual selves, why is it that we are utterly unmindful of our Blissful state and are instead subject to physical and mental pain and suffering?* The answer is, that the Spiritual self has brought on itself this present state (by whatever process it may be) by identifying itself with a transitory bodily vehicle and a restless mind. The Spiritual self being thus identified, feels itself sorry for or delighted at a corresponding unhealthy and unpleasant or healthy and pleasant state of the body and mind. Because of this identification, the Spiritual self is being continually disturbed by their transitory states. To take even the figurative sense of identification: a mother who is in deep identification with her only child suffers and feels intense pain merely by the very hearing of her child's probable or real death, whereas she may feel no such pain if she hears of the death of a neighboring mother's child with whom she has not identified herself. Now we can imagine the consciousness when the identification is real and not figurative. Thus *the sense of identification with the transitory body and restless mind is the source or root-cause of our Spiritual self's misery.*

Identification of the Spiritual self with the body and mind being the primary cause of pain, *we should now turn to a psychological analysis of the immediate or proximate causes of pain and to the distinction between pain, pleasure, and Bliss.*

Because of this identification the Spiritual self seems to have certain tendencies, mental and physical. Desire for the fulfillment of these tendencies creates want, and want produces pain. Now these tendencies or inclinations are either natural or created, natural tendencies producing natural want and created tendencies producing created want. A created want becomes a natural want in time through habit. Of whatever sort the want may be, it gives pain. The more wants we have, the greater the possibilities of pain. For the more wants we have, the more difficult is it to fulfill them, and the more wants remain unfulfilled, the greater is the pain. Increase desires and wants, and pain is also increased. Thus if desire finds no prospect of immediate fulfillment, or finds an obstruction, pain immediately arises. And what is desire? It is nothing but a new condition of "excitation" which the mind puts on itself—a whim of the mind created through company. *Thus desire, or the increase of conditions of "excitation" of the mind, is the source of pain or misery, and also of the mistake of seeking to fulfill wants by first creating and increasing them, and then by trying to satisfy them with objects rather than lessening them from the beginning.*

It might appear that pain is sometimes produced without the presence of previous desire, for example, pain from a boil. But we should observe here that the desire to remain in a state of health which, consciously or subconsciously, is present in our mind and is crystallized into our physiological organism, is contradicted in the above case by the presence of the unhealthy state, viz., the presence of the boil. Thus when a certain exciting condition of the mind in the form of a desire is not satisfied or removed, pain results.

As desire, I have pointed out, leads to pain, so it leads also to pleasure, the only difference being that in the first case want involved in desire is not satisfied, while in the second case want involved in desire seems to be satisfied by the presence of external objects. But this pleasurable experience, resulting from the fulfillment of the want by objects, does not remain long but dies away, and we retain only the memory of the objects that seemed to have removed the want. Hence, in future, desire for those objects brought in by memory revives, and there arises a feeling of want which, if unfulfilled, again leads to pain.

Pleasure is a double consciousness—made up of an "excitation" consciousness of possession of the thing desired and of the consciousness that pain for want of the thing is felt no more. That is, there is an element of both feeling and thought in it. This latter *contrast consciousness*, i.e., the entire consciousness (how much pain I felt when I did not have the thing and how I now have no pain, as I have got the thing I wanted), is what mainly constitutes for men the charm of pleasure. Hence we see that consciousness of want precedes—and consciousness of the want being fulfilled enters into—pleasurable consciousness. Thus it is want and the fulfillment of want with which the pleasure consciousness is concerned. It is mind that creates want and fulfills it.

It is a great mistake to regard a certain object as pleasurable in itself and to store the idea of it in the mind in the hope of fulfilling a want by its actual presence in the future. If objects were pleasurable in themselves, then the same dress or food would always please every one, which is not the case. What is called *pleasure* is a creation of the mind—*it is a deluding, "excitation" consciousness, depending upon the satisfaction of the preceding state of desire and upon present contrast consciousness.* The more a thing is thought to excite pleasurable consciousness and the more the want of it is harbored in the mind, the more the possibility of hankering after the thing itself the presence of which is thought to bring a pleasurable consciousness and its absence a sense of want. Both of these states of consciousness lead ultimately to pain. So if we are to really lessen pain, we are, as far as possible, to free the mind gradually from all desire and sense of want. If desire for a particular thing, supposed to remove the want, is banished, deluding, "excitation" consciousness of pleasure does not arise, even if the thing is somehow present before us. But instead of lessening or decreasing the sense of want, we habitually increase it and create new and various wants for the satisfying of one, resulting in a desire to fulfill them all. For instance, to avoid the want of money we start a business. In order to carry on the business we have to pay attention to thousands of wants and necessities that the carrying on of a business entails. Each want and necessity in turn involves other wants and more attention, and so on. Thus we see that the original pain involved in want of money is a thousand times multiplied by the creation of other wants and interests. Of course it is not meant that the running of a business or earning of money is bad or absolutely unnecessary. The point is that the desire to create greater and greater wants is bad.

If in undertaking to earn money for some end we make money our end, our madness begins. For the means becomes the end and the real end is lost sight of. And so again our misery commences. The question may be—how does our misery begin? The answer is this. In this world every one has his duties to perform. Let us, for the sake of convenience, review the former instance. The family man has to earn money to support his family, which means the doing away of his wants and those of his family. To earn money, let us suppose he starts a business and begins to attend to the details that will make it possible and successful. Now what ordinarily happens after a time? The business goes on successfully and money perhaps rapidly accumulates until it is much more than is necessary for the fulfillment of his wants and those of his family. Now one of two things happens. Either money comes to be earned for its own sake and a peculiar pleasure comes to be felt in hoarding, or it may happen that the hobby of running this business for its own sake persists or increases the more. We see that in either case the means of quelling original wants—which was the end—has become an end in itself—money or business has become the end. Or it may happen that new and unnecessary wants are created and an effort is made to meet them with things. In any case our sole attention drifts away from Bliss (which we, by nature, mistake for pleasure and the latter becomes our end). Then the purpose for which we apparently started business becomes secondary to the creation or increase of conditions or means. And at the root of creation or increase of conditions or means there is a desire for them which is an excitation or feeling, and also a mental picture of the past when these conditions gave rise to pleasure. Naturally the desire seeks fulfillment by the presence of these conditions; when it is fulfilled, pleasure arises, when not fulfilled, pain arises. And because pleasure, as we remarked already, is born of desire and is connected with transitory things, it leads to excitation and pain when there is a disappearance of those things. That is how our misery commences. To put it briefly: from the original purpose of the business, which was the removal of physical wants, we turn to the means,—either to the business itself or to the hoarding of wealth coming out of it,—or sometimes to the creation of new wants, and because we find pleasure in these we are drawn away to pain, which, as we pointed out, is always an indirect outcome of pleasure.

What is true of the earning of money is also true of every action of the world. *Whenever we forget our true end—the attainment of Bliss or the state, condition, or mode of living eventually leading to it—and direct our sole attention to the things which are mistakenly thought to be the means or conditions of Bliss, and turn them into ends, our wants, desires, excitations go on increasing, and we are started on the road to misery or pain.* We should never forget our goal. We should put a hedge round our wants. We should not go on increasing them from more to more, for that will bring misery in the end. I do not mean, however, that we should not satisfy necessary wants, arising out of our relation to the whole world, and become idle dreamers and idealists, ignoring our own essential part in promoting human progress.

To sum up: pain results from desire, and in an indirect way also from pleasure, which stands as a will-o'-the-wisp to lure people away into the mire of wants to make them ever miserable.

Thus we see desire is the root of all misery, which arises out of the sense of identification of our "self" with mind and body. *So what we should do is to kill attachment by doing away with the sense of identification.* We should break the cord of attachment and identification only. We should play our parts, as appointed by the Great Stage Manager, on the stage of the world with our whole mind, intellect, and body, inwardly as unaffected or unruffled by pleasure and pain consciousness as are the players on an ordinary stage. When there is dispassion and severing of identification, Bliss-consciousness arises in us. As long as you are human you can not but have desires. Being human, how then can you realize your divinity? First rationalize your desires, then stimulate your desire for nobler things, all the while trying to attain Bliss-consciousness. You will feel that the cord of your individual attachment to those desires is being automatically snapped. That is to say, from that calm center of Bliss you will ultimately learn to *disown* your own desires and feel them as being urged in you by a great Law. So Jesus Christ said, "Let Thy will be done, O Father, not my own."

When I say that to attain *Bliss* is the universal end of Religion, I do not mean by Bliss what is usually called pleasure, or that intellectual satisfaction which arises from the fulfillment of desire and want and which is mixed with an excitation, as when we say we are pleasurably excited. In Bliss there is no excitement, nor is it a contrast consciousness that "my pain or want has been removed by the presence of such and such objects." It is a consciousness of perfect tranquillity—a consciousness of our calm nature unpolluted by the intruding consciousness that pain is no more. An illustration will make the thing clear. I have a boil, and feel pain; when cured I feel pleasure. This pleasurable consciousness consists of an "excitation" or feeling, and a contrast thought-consciousness that I am no longer feeling the pain of the boil. Now the man who has attained Bliss, though having had a boil on his leg, will feel, when cured, that his state of tranquillity had neither been disturbed, when the boil was, nor regained when it was cured. He feels that he passed through a pain-pleasure universe with which he really has no connection or which can neither disturb nor heighten the tranquil or blissful state which flows on without ceasing. This state of Bliss is free from both inclinations and excitement involved in pleasure or this pain.

There is a positive and a negative aspect in Bliss-consciousness. The negative aspect is the absence of pleasure-pain consciousness; the positive one is the transcendental state of a superior calm including within itself the consciousness of a great expansion and that of "all in One and One in all." It has its degrees. An earnest truth-seeker gets a little taste of it, a seer or a prophet is filled with it.

Pleasure and pain having their origin in desire and want, it should be our duty, if we wish to attain Bliss, to banish desire and what seriously fans desire. If all our improvements—scientific, social, and political—are guided by this one common universal end,—removal of pain,—why should we bring in a foreign something—pleasure—and forget to be durably fixed in what is tranquillity or Bliss? He who enjoys the pleasure of health will inevitably sometimes feel the pain due to ill-health, because pleasure depends upon a condition of the mind, viz., the idea of health. To have good health is not bad nor is it wrong to seek it. But to have attachment to it, to be pleasurably or painfully affected by it, is what is objected to. For to be so means entertaining desire, which will lead to misery. We must seek health not for the pleasure in it but because it makes the performance of duties and the attainment of our goal possible. It will some time or other be contradicted by the opposing condition, viz., ill-health. But Bliss depends upon no particular condition, external or internal. *It is a native state of the spirit.* Therefore it has no fear of being contradicted by the opposing condition. It will flow on continually for ever, in defeat or success, in health or disease, in opulence or poverty.

Now the above psychological discussion about pain, pleasure, and Bliss, with the help of the following two examples, will make clear my conception of the highest common necessity and of the God-head, which was touched upon incidentally at the beginning. We remarked at the outset that if we made a close observation of the actions of men, we should see that the one fundamental and universal motive for which man acts is the permanent avoidance of pain and the consequent attainment of Bliss, or God. The first part of the motive, i.e., the permanent avoidance of pain, is something we can not deny, if we observe the motives of all the best and worst actions performed in the world. Take the case of a person who wishes to commit suicide and that of a truly religious man who has dispassion for the things of the world. There can be no doubt about the fact that both of these men are trying to get rid of the pain which is troubling them. Both are trying to permanently put an end to pain. Whether they are successful or not is a different question, but so far as their motives are concerned there is unity. (The question of the means of permanently doing away with pain will be discussed later on.) But are all actions in this world *directly* prompted by the desire for the attainment of permanent Bliss, or God, the second part of the common motive for all actions? Does the debauchee have for his immediate motive the attainment of Bliss? Hardly. The reason for this we pointed out in our discussion about pleasure and Bliss. We found that because of the identification of the Spiritual self with the body it has got into the habit of indulging in desires and the consequent creation of wants. These desires and wants lead to pain, if not fulfilled—and to pleasure, if fulfilled—by objects. But here occurs a fatal error on the part of man. When a want is fulfilled man gets a pleasurable excitement and fixes his eye, through a sad mistake, solely upon the objects which create this excitement, and supposes them to be the main causes of his pleasure. He entirely forgets that he had formerly an excitation in the form of desire or want in his own mind, and that later he had another excitation in his mind superseding the first one, in the form of pleasure which the coming of objects seems to produce. So, as a matter of fact, one excitation arose in the mind and was superseded by another in the same mind.

Outward objects are only the occasions—they are not causes. They are mistakenly thought to produce pleasure. Desire for delicacies by a poor person can be satisfied by an ordinary sweetmeat, and this fulfillment will give rise to pleasure. But the desire for delicacies on the part of a rich person can perhaps be satisfied only by the best of Christmas cake, and the fulfillment will also give the *same amount of* pleasure. *Then does pleasure depend on outward objects, or on the state of mind? Surely the latter.* But pleasure, as we said, is an excitation. Therefore it is never justifiable to drive away the excitation in desire by another excitation, viz., that felt in pleasure. Because we do this our excitations never end, and so our pain and misery never cease. What we should do is to *set at rest* the excitation that is in desire and not to fan or continue it by excitation in pleasure. This setting at rest is rendered possible, in an effective way, only by Bliss-consciousness which is not callousness but a superior stage of indifference to both pain and pleasure. *Every human being is seeking to attain Bliss by fulfilling desire, but he mistakenly stops at pleasure, and so his desires never end, and he is swept away into the whirlpool of pain.*

Pleasure is a dangerous will-o'-the-wisp. And yet it is this pleasurable association that becomes our motive for future actions. But alas! this has proved to be as deceptive as the mirage in a desert. Since pleasure, as was said before, consists of an excitation-consciousness plus a contrast-consciousness that the pain is now no more, we prepare ourselves, when we aim at it instead of at Bliss, for running headlong into that cycle of empirical existence which brings pleasure and pain in never-ending succession. We fall into horrible distress because of the change in our angle of vision from Bliss to pleasure, which latter crops up in place of the former. Thus we see that though the true aim of mankind is the avoidance of pain and the attainment of Bliss, yet owing to a fatal error man, though trying to avoid pain, *pursues a deluding something named pleasure, mistaking it for Bliss.* That the attainment of Bliss and not pleasure is the Universal and Highest Necessity is indirectly proved by the fact that man is never satisfied with one object of pleasure. He always flies from one to another. From money to dress, from dress to property, thence to conjugal pleasure—there is a restless continuity. And so he is constantly falling into pain, even if he wishes to avoid it, by the adoption of what he deems proper means. Yet an unknown and unsatisfied craving seems ever to remain in his heart.

But a religious man (the second example which I proposed to show) always wishes to adopt proper religious means by which he can come in contact with Bliss-God.

Of course when I say that God is Bliss, I

mean also that He is Ever-existent and that He is also *conscious* of His Blissful Existence. And when we wish Eternal Bliss or God, it is implied that with Bliss we also wish Eternal, Immortal, Unchangeable, Ever-conscious Existence. That all of us, from the highest to the lowest, desire to be in Bliss has been proved *a priori*, and by a consideration of the motives and acts of men. To repeat the argument in a slightly different way: suppose some Higher Being should come to us and say to all people of the world, "You creatures of the world! I will give you eternal sorrows and misery along with eternal existence; will you take that?" Would any one like the prospect? Not one. All want eternal Bliss (Anandam) along with eternal existence (Sat). As a matter of fact, consideration of the motives of the world also shows there is no one but would like to have Bliss or Anandam. Similarly, no one likes the prospect of immediate annihilation; if it is suggested, we shudder at the idea. All desire to exist permanently (Sat). But if we were given eternal existence without the consciousness of that existence, we would reject that. For who is there that would embrace existence in sleep? None. We all want conscious existence. Furthermore, we want Blissful Conscious Existence. We want Satchidanandam—that is God. But for a pragmatical consideration only we emphasize the Blissful aspect of God and our motive for Bliss, leaving out two other aspects —Sat and Chit, i.e., Conscious Existence. Also other aspects of Him are not dwelt on here.

Now, what is *God?* If God be something other than Bliss, and His contact produces in us no Bliss, or produces in us only pain, or if His contact does not drive pain away from us, should we want Him? No. If God is something useless to us, we want Him not. What is the use of a God who remains always unknown and whose presence is not *inwardly* manifest to us at least in some circumstance in our life? Whatever conception of God we form by the exercise of reason or intellect, viz., Transcendant, Immanent, etc., will always remain vague and indistinct unless really felt as such. In fact, we keep God at a safe distance, conceiving Him sometimes as a mere Personal Being, and then again *theoretically* thinking Him to be within us. It is because of this vagueness in our idea and experience concerning God that we are not able to grasp the real necessity of God and the pragmatical value of Religion. This colorless theory or idea does not bring conviction to us. It can not change our lives, influence our conduct in an appreciable way, or *make us try to know God.*

What does "Universal Religion" say about God? It says that the *proof of the existence of God lies in ourselves.* It is an inner experience. Recall to your mind at least some moment in your life in prayer or worship when you felt that the trammels of your body had nearly vanished, that the duality of experience—

pleasure and pain, petty love and hate, etc.—had almost receded from your mind. Pure Bliss and tranquillity had been welling up in your heart and you were enjoying an unruffled calm—Bliss and contentment. Though this kind of higher experience does not often come to all, yet there can be no doubt of the fact that all men, some time or other, in prayer or in mood of worship or meditation, perceive it in a less marked degree, at least. Is this not a proof of the existence of God? *What other direct proof than the existence of Bliss in ourselves in real prayer or worship can we give of the existence and nature of God?* Though there is the cosmological proof of the existence of God,—from effect we rise to cause, from the world to the world-maker,—and there is the teleological proof as well, from the telos (plan, adaptation) in the world, we rise to the Supreme Intelligence that makes the plan and adaptation. There is also the moral proof—from conscience and the sense of perfection we rise to the Perfect Being to whom our responsibility is due. Still, we should admit that these proofs are more or less the products of inference. We can not have full or direct knowledge of God through the limited powers of the intellect. Intellect gives only a partial and indirect view of things. To view a thing intellectually is not to see it by being one with it: it is to view it by being apart from it. But Intuition, which we shall later explain, is the direct grasp of truth. It is in this Intuition that Bliss-consciousness, or God-consciousness, is realized.

There is not a shadow of doubt as to the absolute identity of Bliss-consciousness and God-consciousness, because when we have that Bliss-consciousness we feel that our narrow individuality has been transformed and that we have risen above the duality of petty love and hate, pleasure and pain, etc., and have attained a level from which the painfulness and worthlessness of empirical consciousness become glaringly apparent. And we also feel an inward expansion and all-embracing sympathy for all things. The tumults of the world die away, excitements disappear, and the "all in One and One in all" consciousness seems to dawn upon us. A glorious vision of light appears. All imperfections, all angularities, sink into nothingness. We seem to be translated into another region, the fountainhead of perennial Bliss, the starting point of one unending continuity. Is not Bliss-consciousness, then, the same as God-consciousness, in which (God-consciousness) the above states of realization seem obvious? It is evident, then, that God cannot be better conceived than as Bliss coming within the range of every one's calm-experience. No longer will God be a supposition, to be theorized over. Is this not a nobler conception of God? He is perceived as manifesting Himself in our hearts in the form of Bliss in meditation—in prayerful or worshipful mood. *If we conceive of God in this way, i. e., as Bliss, then and then only can we make Religion universally necessary.* For no one can deny that he wishes to get Bliss, and if he wishes to get Bliss in the proper way, he is going to be religious through approaching and feeling God, who is described as very close to his heart as Bliss.

This Bliss-consciousness or God-consciousness can pervade all our actions and moods, if we but let it. If we can get firm hold of this, we shall be able to judge the relative religious worth of every minor action and motive on this earth. If we are once convinced that the attainment of this Bliss-consciousness is our Religion, our goal, our ultimate end, then all doubts as to the meaning of multifarious teachings, injunctions, and prohibitions of the different faiths of the world will disappear. Everything will be interpreted in the light of the stage of growth for which it is prescribed. Truth will shine out, the mystery of existence will be solved, and a light will be thrown upon the details of our lives, with their various actions and motives. We shall be able to separate the naked truth from the outward appendages of religious doctrines and see the worthlessness of conventions that so often mislead men and create differences between them. Further, if religion is understood in this way there is no man in the world—be he a boy, youth, or an old person—who can not practise it, whatever may be the station of life to which he belongs, be it student or professional life, or be he a lawyer, doctor, carpenter, brazier, scholar, or philanthropist. If to abolish the sense of want and attain Bliss is Religion, who is there that is not trying to be religious and will not try to be so in a greater degree, if proper methods are pointed out. Herein does not arise the question of the variety of religions—that of Christ, of Mahomet, or of the Hindus. Every one in the world is inevitably trying to be religious, and can seek to be more completely so by the adoption of proper means.

There is no distinction here of caste or creed, sect or faith, dress or clime, age or sex, profession or position. For this Religion is Universal.

If you said that all the people of the world ought to accept the Lord Krishna as their God, would all the Christians and the Mahomedans accept that? If you asked every one to take Jesus as their Lord, would all the Hindus and Mahomedans do that? And if again you bade all accept Mahomet as their Lord, would all the Christians and Hindus agree to that? But if you say, "Oh, my Christian, Mahomedan and Hindu Brethren, your Lord God is Ever-Blissful Conscious Existence (Being)," will they not accept this? Can they possibly reject it? Will they not demand Him as the only One who can put an end to all their miseries?

Nor can one escape this conclusion by saying that Christians, Hindus, or Mahomedans do not conceive Jesus, Krishna, or

Mahomet respectively as their Lord God,—they are thought to be only the standard-bearers of God, the human incarnations of divinity. What if one thinks that way? It is not the physical body of Jesus, Krishna, or Mahomet that we are primarily interested in, nor are we so much concerned with the historical place they occupy. Nor are they immemorable to us because of their different and interesting ways of preaching God. We revere them because they knew and felt God. It is that fact that interests us in their historical existence and in their manifold ways of expressing the truth. They might or might not be on the same plane. Let the hard-shelled theologians and difference-hunters in religion fight over that question eternally and vainly. But did they not belong to a more or less close family of God? Did they not all realize God as Bliss and reveal real blessedness as true godliness? Is not that a sufficient bond of unity among them,—let alone other aspects of Godhead and truth they might have realized and expressed. Shouldn't a Christian, a Hindu, and a Mahomedan find a mutual interest in each other's prophets, inasmuch as each of them cherished in his heart God-consciousness as primarily Superior Bliss-consciousness? As God unites all religions, is it not the conception and realization of Him as Bliss, if not anything else, that unites the consciousness of the prophets of all religions?*

One should not think that this conception of God is too abstract, having nothing to do with our spiritual hopes and aspirations, which require the conception of God as a Personal Being. It is not the conception of an Imper-

* Bliss-consciousness is also stressed in so-called atheistic religions,—such as Buddhism. The Buddhistic "Nirvana" is not, as mistakenly supposed by Western writers, a "blowing out of light," an extinction of existence. It is rather the stage where narrow individuality is blotted out and transcendant calm in universality is reached. This is exactly what comes of higher Bliss-consciousness, though the name of God is not attached to it by the Buddhist.

sonal Being, as commonly understood, nor that of a Personal Being, as narrowly conceived. God is not a Person, as are we in our narrowness. Our being, consciousness, feeling, volition have but a shadow of resemblance to His Being (Existence), Consciousness, and Anandam. He is a Person in the transcendental sense. Our being, consciousness, feeling are limited and empirical; His are unlimited and transcendental. Nor should He be thought of as Abstract, Absolute, Impersonal, Unconditional, Remote, and beyond the reach of all experience—even our inner one. He, as I have remarked, comes within the calm experience of men. It is in Bliss-consciousness that we realize Him. There can be no other direct proof of His existence. *It is in Him as Bliss that our spiritual hopes and aspirations find fulfillment—our devotion and love find an object.* No other conception of a Personal Being who is nothing but ourselves magnified is required for us. God may be or become anything—Personal, Impersonal, All-merciful, Omnipotent, etc., etc. What we say is that we do not require to take note of these. *Whatever conception we have put forth exactly suits our purposes, our hopes, our aspirations, and our perfection.*

Nor should we think that this conception of God will make us dreamy idealists, severing our connection with the duties and responsibilities, joys and sorrows, of this practical world. If God is Bliss and if we seek Bliss to know Him, we *can not* neglect the duties and responsibilities of the world. In the performance of them we can still feel Bliss, for it is beyond them, and so they can not affect it. We transcend the joys and sorrows of the world in Bliss, but we do not transcend the duties and responsibilities in the sense of neglecting them. For in doing everything—eating, drinking, seeing, hearing, feeling, smelling, tasting, sorrowing, feeling pleasure, performing every minute duty of the world—we do nothing, we eat, drink, see, hear, feel, smell, taste nothing,—we feel no sorrow nor pleasure. We remain unattached; all actions flow from our nature—that is human. We, bathed in an unending flow of Bliss, feel our "self" to be the *dispassionate seer* of all our actions. Our narrow egoism vanishes, the All-Ego dawns, and Bliss spreads through our being. We feel that we are playing our appointed parts on the stage of the world, without being *inwardly* affected by the weal and woe, love and hate, that the playing of a part involves.

Verily, in all respects the world can be likened to a stage. The stage manager chooses people to help him in the enactment of a certain play. He allots particular parts to particular persons—all of them work according to his directions. One the stage manager makes a king, one a minister, one a servant, another the hero, and so on. One has to play a sorrowful part, another a joyful one. If each one plays his part according to the directions of the stage manager, then the play, with all its diversities of comical, serious, sorrowful parts, becomes successful. Even the insignificant parts have their indispensable places in the play. The success of the play lies in the perfect playing out of each part. Each actor plays his part of sorrow or pleasure realistically, and to all outward appearances seems to be affected by it; but inwardly he remains untouched by it or by the passions he portrays—love, hate, desire, malice, glory, humility. But if any actor, in the playing of a part, identified himself with a certain situation or a particular feeling expressed in the play and lost his own individuality, he would be thought foolish, to say the least. A story will bring out the latter point clearly.

Once in the house of a rich man the play of Ramayan was staged. In the course of the play it was found that the man who should play the part of Hunuman (monkey), the attendant-friend of Ram, was missing. In his perplexity the stage manager seized upon an ugly simpleton, Nilkamal by name, and sought to make him enact the part of *Hunuman.* Nilkamal at first refused, but was forced to appear on the stage. His ugly appearance excited loud laughter among the spectators and they began to shout in merriment, "*Hunuman, Hunuman!*" Nilkamal could hardly bear this. He forgot that it was a play, and bawled out in real exasperation and disgust, "Why, Sirs, do you call me *Hunuman?* Why do you laugh? I am not a *Hunuman.* The stage manager made me come out here this way." This excited further roars of laughter from the audience and they began to shout in right earnest, "*Hunuman, Hunuman!*" Nilkamal, mad with rage and disgust, not understanding the meaning of all this, retired from the stage exclaiming, "I am not a *Hunuman;* how can I be made a *Hunuman.*"

Nilkamal failed to distinguish between the real *Hunuman* and the *Hunuman* of the play. In this world our lives are nothing but plays. But alas! we identify ourselves with the play, and hence feel disgust, sorrow, pleasure, etc. We forget the direction and injunction of the Great Stage Manager. In the act of living our lives—playing our parts—we feel as real all our sorrows and pleasures, loves and hates —in a word, we become attached, affected. This play of the world is without beginning and end. Every one must play his part, as assigned by the Great Stage Manager, ungrudgingly; must play for the sake of the play only; must act sorrowful when playing sorrowful parts, or pleased when playing pleasurable parts, but should never be inwardly *identified with the play*—with its sorrows and pleasures, loves and hates. Nor should one wish to play another's part. If every one aspires to play the role of a king, the play will be impossible.

He who has attained to the *superior* stage of Bliss-consciousness will *feel* the world to be a stage and play out his part as best he can, feeling it as such, remembering the Great Stage Manager (God), and knowing and feeling His nature in its every aspect — His plan and direction.

NOTE.—The derivation of the word "religion" from *religare*, to bind (see page 10) has been adopted by St. Augustine, Lactantius, Lucretius, and Servius. (See Enc. Brit., 11th Edition.)

CHAPTER II

Four Fundamental Religious Methods

We have seen in the last chapter that the identification of the Spiritual self with body and mind is the fundamental cause of our pain, suffering, and limitations, and that because of this identification we feel such excitations as pain and pleasure, and are almost blind to the state of Bliss, or God-consciousness. We have also seen that religion essentially consists in the permanent avoidance of such pain and in the attainment of pure Bliss, or God.

As the sun's true image cannot be perceived in the surface of moving water, so the true blissful nature of the Spiritual self—the reflection of the Universal Spirit—cannot be understood owing to the waves of disquietude that arise from identification of the self with the changing states of the body and mind.

As the moving waters distort the true image of the sun, so does the disturbed state of the mind, through identification, distort the true, Ever-Blissful nature of our own self.

The purpose of this chapter is to discuss the easiest, most rational, and most fundamental methods (practical for all) that will free the Ever-Blissful, Spiritual self from its baneful connection and identification with the transitory body and mind, thus causing it to permanently avoid pain and attain Bliss, which constitutes Religion. Therefore the fundamental methods to be considered are religious and involve religious actions, because only by means of these can the Spiritual self be freed from the body and mind and thus from pain, and be made to attain permanent Bliss, or God.

A general idea of the religious method is given in one, among a great many, of Christ's teachings. He says, "Unless ye have lifted up the Son of man, ye can not enter into the kingdom of God." The "Son of man" means the progeny of man, i.e., *the body* which is born out of another human body. It may seem to us that "Son of man" means something other than this—that it means Christ. Granting this, we are then to interpret the next saying of Christ, "The Son of man shall be delivered unto the Gentiles and He shall be crucified," as meaning that Christ, the Eternal Spirit, was to be crucified by material nails and His Spirit destroyed, an explanation which is obviously absurd; for it was the material body only, in which the Spirit of Christ was clothed, that could possibly be crucified, not the Spirit. We can explain the first quoted saying of Christ in this way: unless we can *transcend* the body and realize ourselves as spirit, we cannot enter into the kingdom or state of that Universal Spirit. We find an echo of this in a Sanskrit couplet of the Oriental scriptures: "If thou canst transcend the body and perceive thyself as spirit, thou shalt be eternally blissful and free from all pain." (When Christ called himself Son of God, he meant the Universal Spirit dwelling in him.)

Now there are *four* fundamental, universal religious methods which, if followed in daily life, will in time liberate the Spiritual self from the trammels of its bodily and mental vehicles. *Under these four classes* of religious methods I include all the possible religious practices that have ever been enjoined by any saint or savant or any prophet of God. Religious practices are inculcated by prophets in the form of doctrines. Men of limited intellect, failing to interpret the true import of these doctrines, accept their exoteric or outer meaning and gradually fall into forms, conventions, and rigid practices. This is the origin of sectarianism. Rest from work on the sabbath day was interpreted by the Jews to mean rest from all work—even religious work. This is the danger to men of limited understanding.

We should remember that we are not made for the sabbath, but that the sabbath is made for us; we are not made for rules, rules are made for us—they change as circumstances change. We are to hold to the essence of a rule, not dogmatically to its form. Change of forms and customs constitutes for many a change from one religion to another. But the deepest import of all the doctrines of all the different prophets is often the same. Most men do not understand this.

But there is equal danger in the case of the intellectually great. They try to know the Highest Truth by the exercise of the intellect only. But the Highest Truth can be known only by realization. Realization is something other than mere understanding. We could not possibly understand the sweetness of sugar if we had not tasted it. Just so, religious knowledge is drawn from the deepest experience of one's own soul. This we often forget when we seek to learn about God, religious dogmas, and morality. We do not seek to know these through inner religious experience. It is a pity that men of great intellectual power, successful in their use of reason in the way of discovering the deep truths of the natural sciences, etc., think that they will also be able to grasp intellectually the highest religious and moral truths. It is also a pity that the intellect or reason of these men, instead of being a help, is found to be a bar to their comprehension of the Highest Truth by the only means possible—living it in one's life.

Let us consider the four methods characterizing religious growth.

I. Intellectual Method. The commonly-adopted, natural method, not so effective in realizing the end.

Intellectual development and progression has been natural and hence common to all rational beings. It is our self-conscious understanding which differentiates us from the lower animals, that are conscious but not self-conscious. In the grades and processes of evolution we see that this consciousness gradually becomes self-consciousness—from animal consciousness self-consciousness arises. The consciousness gradually tries to free itself and tries to know itself by itself, and it is thus changed into self-consciousness. This change is due to an evolutional necessity, and the universal urge toward intellectual pursuits is due to this evolutional tendency. The Spiritual self, identified with various degrees and sorts of bodily and mental states, tries gradually and naturally to return to itself through itself. The development of the conscious thought-process is one of the methods which the Spiritual self adopts to rise above the trammels of body and mind. The effort of the Spiritual self to return to itself—its lost condition—through the development of thought-process is natural. This is the process of the world. The Universal Spirit expresses itself in different grades of development, from lower to higher. In stone and earth there is no life or consciousness. In trees there is vegetative growth, an approach to life, yet no full-grown life and no conscious thought-process at all. In animals there is life and also consciousness of life. In man—the culmination point—there is life, consciousness of it, and also consciousness of the *Self* (i.e., Self-consciousness). Hence it is natural for man to develop himself through thinking and reasoning, by deep study of books, by original research work, and by laborious investigations into causes and effects in the natural world. The more deeply a man engages in thought-processes, the more he can be said to be utilizing the *method* by which he has come to be what he is in the course of the world-evolution process (i.e., the method by which consciousness develops into Self-consciousness) and the nearer, knowingly or unknowingly, he approaches the Self. *For in thought we rise above the body. The deliberate following of this method will bring about sure results.* Exercise of thought in study, etc., solely for the acquirement of knowledge of a certain thing, though to some extent improving the self-consciousness, is not so effective as that thought-process which *has as its sole object the transcending of the body and seeing the truth.*

One of the defects of this method is that it is a very *slow* process for the Spiritual self to thus realize itself. It may involve a good deal of time. While the Spiritual self begins to apprehend self-consciousness by this method, still it is always engaged with a series of passing mental thoughts with which it *has no relation.* Tranquillity of the spirit is something beyond thought or bodily sensation, though when once attained it overflows both.

II. DEVOTIONAL METHOD. This consists in fixing the attention of the Spiritual self on one object of thought, rather than on different series of thoughts and on different subjects, as in the intellectual method. Under this method are included all forms of worship (such as prayer, *from which we must eliminate all thoughts of worldly things*), or objects of reverence. The Spiritual self must fix its attention deeply on whatsoever it chooses to concentrate on. It may be any thing that it likes. The Spiritual self may create a Personal God, an Impersonal Omnipresent God, or any other thing. It must simply concentrate on one subject of thought in *good earnest.*

By this process the Spiritual self becomes gradually freed from the disturbances of vagrant thoughts—the second series of disturbances—and gets time and opportunity to think itself in itself. When we *pray* earnestly, we forget all bodily sensations and drive away all intruding thoughts that try to engage our attention.

The deeper our prayer, the more intense is the satisfaction felt, and this becomes the criterion by which we measure how far we have approached Bliss-God. As the bodily sensations are left behind and the vagrant thoughts are checked, the superiority of this over the foregoing method becomes manifest.

However, this method presents certain defects and difficulties. Owing to the long-continued attachment and slavery of the Spiritual self to the body—to this deep-rooted bad habit—it ineffectually tries to turn its attention away from the sphere of bodily and mental sensations. However much one may wish to pray or engage in any form of worship with one's whole heart, one's attention is mercilessly invaded by the raiding bodily sensations and vagrant thoughts brought in by memory. In prayer we are often wholly engrossed in the consideration of the circumstances favorable to it, or we are too ready to remove any of our disturbing bodily discomforts. In spite of all our conscious efforts our bad habit, which has become a second nature to us, lords it over the self's wishes. In spite of our wish, our mind becomes restless. "Wherever your mind shall be there shall your heart be also," and "Pray God with all thy heart." Instead, we generally pray to God with our mind and heart occupied with bodily and mental disturbances. Let us look for a more effective way by which our self's effort may be made easier and be more greatly helped.

III. Meditation Method. This and the next method are purely scientific, involving a practical course of training, and are prescribed by great savants who have realized the truth personally in their own lives. I myself learned them from one of these. There is nothing of mystery in them, or anything to be dreaded as harmful. They are very easy, if one is properly acquainted with them. They will be found to be universally true. Practically-felt knowledge is the best proof of their validity and pragmatic utility.

By undergoing regularly the processes of meditation till they become a habit, we can bring upon ourselves a state of *conscious sleep*. We generally experience this calm and pleasurable tranquil state just when we are falling into deep sleep and approaching unconsciousness, or rising from it and approaching consciousness. In this state of conscious sleep we become free from all thoughts and outer bodily sensations, and the self gets time to think of itself—it comes into the blissful state from time to time, according to the depth and frequency of its practice of meditation. In this state we are utterly forgetful of and free from all bodily and mental disturbances which divert the self's attention. By this process of meditation the outer organs are controlled by the controlling of the voluntary nerves, as in sleep.

But the process of meditation has also its *drawbacks and defects*. By this process, just as in sleep, we learn to control only our outer organs, the only difference being that in sleep the outer organs are automatically controlled, while in meditation, on the contrary, the outer organs are voluntarily controlled. This produces a state of "conscious sleep." The Spiritual self then experiences this state of conscious sleep, being continually disturbed by the involuntary and internal organs, e.g., lungs, heart, and other organs which we mistakenly suppose to be beyond control.*

We must look for a better method than this, for so long as the Spiritual self can not at will shut out all *bodily sensations, even interior ones, which are the occasions of the rise of thought,* but remains vulnerable to these disturbances, it can have no hope of final rest nor time or opportunity to know itself.

IV. Organic, Scientific Method. St. Paul said: "*I die daily*" (1 Cor. 15, 31). By

*We never know or learn how to give rest to these internal organs. Because we suppose them to be beyond control, they get overworked and suddenly stop, which stoppage we term "Death," or the "Eternal or Great Sleep."

this he meant that he knew the process of controlling the internal organs and could voluntarily free his Spiritual self from the body and mind, the sudden freedom of which, due to the wearing out of this gross body and mind, is termed *death*. Now by undergoing a practical and regular course of training in this scientific method the self can be felt as being separated from the body.

I will give only a general idea of the process and the true scientific theory on which it is based. I set it down here from my own experience. I can say it will be found to be universally true. And I *can also safely say that Bliss, which is, as I pointed out, our ultimate end, is felt in intense degree in the act of practising this method. The practice of it is itself intensely Blissful—far more purely Blissful,* I venture to say, *than the greatest enjoyment that any of our five senses or the mind can ever afford us.* I do not wish to give any one any other proof of its truth *than is afforded by his own experience.* The more one practises it *with patience* and duration, the more one feels intensely and *durably fixed in Bliss.* Owing to the persistence of bad habits, the consciousness of bodily existence, with all its memories, revives occasionally and fights against that tranquillity. If any one practises regularly and for extended periods, it can be guaranteed that in time he will find himself in a highly super-mental *state of Bliss.* We should not, however, *overwisely* seek to imagine beforehand the possible results to which the process may lead, and then cease practising the method after a short trial.

In order to make real progress the following things are necessary: First, loving attention to the subject to be learned; second, desire to learn and an earnest spirit of inquiry; third, steadfastness until the desired end is attained. If we go only half-way and then, after a short practice, reject it, the desired result will not follow. If novices in spiritual practices try to pre-judge the experience of experts, they will appear as ridiculous as a child who tries to imagine what post-graduate studies would be like. It is a great pity that men will spend their best efforts and time in securing what is needed for worldly existence or in indulging in intellectual controversy over theories, but seem never to think it worth their while to realize and patiently experience in life the truths which not only vivify but impart meaning to it. Misguided efforts can engage their attention longer than well-guided efforts. I have been practising the above-mentioned method for the last 18 years, and the more I do so, the more I feel the joy of a state of permanent and unfailing Bliss. We should bear in mind that the Spiritual self has been in bondage to the body for how many ages we know not. It cannot be freed in one day, nor will short or desultory practice of the method take one to the Supreme State of Bliss or give one control over the internal organs. It will require *patient* practice for a *long, long* time. I guarantee this, however,—that the following of this process will bring the great joy of pure Bliss-consciousness. The more we practise it, the more we get that Blissful state. I wish that, as seekers of Bliss, which all of us are, you should try to experience for yourselves that universal truth which is in all and may be felt by all. This is not an invention of anyone. It is already there. We are simply to discover it.

Do not, until you have tested this truth, look upon what I write with indifference. It may be that you are tired of hearing various theories, none of which has hitherto had any direct bearing on your life. This is no theory, but realized truth. I am trying to give you a general idea of what can be really experienced.

I had the fortune to learn this "Holy, Scientific Truth" from a great saint of India a good many years ago. You may ask why I urge you—why I draw your attention to these facts? Have I any selfish interest? To this I answer in the affirmative. I wish to sell this truth to you with the hope of getting in return pure joy by helping you find your joy in the practice and realization of it.

Now I have to enter into a little physiology, which will enable us to understand the method, at least in a general way. I must describe the work of the main centres and the electrical current that flows from the brain through these centres to the outer and internal organs and keeps them vibrating with life.

There are six main centres through which Pranic Current, Vital Current, or Life Electricity from the brain is discharged throughout the nervous system. These are:

Medulla-centre.	Lumbar-centre.
Cervical-centre.	Sacral-centre.
Dorsal-centre.	Coccygeal-centre.

The brain is the supreme electrical Power-House (supreme centre). All the centres are connected with one another and act under the influence of the supreme centre (brain-cells). The brain-cells discharge life current, or electricity, through these cells, which in turn discharge electricity to the different efferent and afferent nerves which respectively carry motor impulse and sensation of touch, sight, etc. *This electrical flow from the brain is the life of the organism (of its internal and external organs), and it is this electrical medium through which all our sensation reports reach the brain and cause thought disturbances.* The self, if it wishes effectively to shut out the disturbing reports of bodily sensations (which are also the occasions of the rise of the thought-series), must control and concentrate the electrical flow and draw it back from the nervous system as a whole to the seven main centres (including the brain), so that by this process it may give the outer and internal organs perfect rest. In sleep, the electrical conductivity between the brain and the outer organs is partially inhibited, so that ordinary sensations of sound, touch, etc., cannot reach the brain. But because this inhibition is not complete, a sufficiently strong stimulus from without restores this electrical conductivity and is reported to the brain, awakening the person. Yet always in sleep there is a steady electrical flow into the internal organs,—heart, lungs, etc.,—so that they keep on throbbing and working.

As the control of life electricity in sleep is not complete, bodily sensations of discomfort, disease, or strong outside stimuli disturb it. But through a scientific process of control, which is not here described in detail, we can simultaneously control the external and internal organs of the system in a perfect way. That is the ultimate result of practice. But it will take long, long years to attain that perfect control. As after sleep, which is rest, the outer organs are invigorated, so the internal organs, after rest, as a result of the practice of this scientific method, are greatly vitalized, and with the consequent increase in their working power life is prolonged. As we do not fear to go to sleep, lest for the time being the outer organs remain inert, so we ought not fear to practise death, i.e., give rest to the internal organs. Death will then be under our control; for when we think this bodily house is unfit and broken, we shall be able to leave it of our own accord. "The last enemy that shall be destroyed is death." (1 Cor. 15, 26.)

We may describe the process thus: If the main telephone office in a town is permanently connected by wires with different parts of the town, men telephoning from those parts can always, even against the will of the authorities of the main telephone office, send messages to the central office through the medium of the electric current running along the connecting wires. If the main telephone office wishes to stop communication with the different parts, it can turn off the main electrical switch and there will be no flow to the different quarters of the town. Similarly, the scientific method teaches a process enabling us to draw to its central part—spine and brain—the life current distributed throughout the organs and other parts of the body. The process, roughly speaking, lies in magnetizing the spinal column, which contains the seven main centres, with the result that the distributed life electricity is drawn back to the original centres of discharge and is experienced in the form of light. In this state the Spiritual self can consciously free itself from its bodily and mental disturbances. The Spiritual self is, as it were, being disturbed, even against its wish, by the telephone reports from two classes of people—gentlemen (thoughts) and low class people—(bodily sensations). In order to break connection with them it has only to draw away the electricity flowing through the telephone wires to the central battery of its house by turning off the switch (i.e., practise the fourth method), in order to enjoy relief.

Attention is the great *director and discharger of energy.* It is the active cause of the discharge of the electrical life current from the brain to the sensory and motor nerves. For example, we drive away a troublesome fly by discharging, through the power of attention, the proper electrical current along the motor nerves, thereby producing the desired movements. I cite this to give an idea of the power by which the electrical flow of the system can be controlled and drawn back to its seven centres. It is of these seven star-like centres and their mystery that we find mention even in the chapter on revelation in the Bible. St. John experienced these seven centres as seven stars while he was in the spirit. "The mystery of the seven stars, which thou sawest, write them in a book."—Revelation 1: 19, 20. It should be noted that when I say the electrical flow of the body is controlled, I mean all electrical currents, whether flowing voluntarily or involuntarily.

In conclusion I wish to describe the nature of the states which emerge when the electrical flow is *completely* controlled. In the beginning a most attractive sensation is felt in the course of magnetizing the spinal column. But continued and long practice will bring about a state of conscious Bliss which counteracts the exciting state of our body-consciousness. *This blissful state has been described as our universal aim and highest necessity, because in it we are really conscious of God, or Bliss,* and feel the expansion of our real selves. The more frequently this is experienced, the more our narrow individuality falls away, the sooner the state of universality is reached, and the closer and more direct is our touch with what we know as God. Religion is really nothing but the merging of our individuality in universality. Therefore, in the consciousness of this Blissful state we ascend the steps of

Religion. We leave the noxious atmosphere of the senses and vagrant thoughts and come to a region of Heavenly Bliss. We learn by this process what will be found to be universally true. When by constant practice the consciousness of this Blissful state of our Spiritual self becomes real we find ourselves always in the Holy presence of the Blissful God in us. We discharge our duties better, having an eye more for the duties themselves than for our "egoism" and the pleasure-pain-consciousness rising therefrom. Then we can solve the mystery of existence and impart real meaning to what is known as life.

Underlying all the so-called Religions—Christianity, Mahomedanism, Hinduism—there is one truth remaining, viz., that unless you know yourself as spirit,—as the fountain-head of Bliss, separate from body and mind,—your existence is devoid of meaning and your life is akin to that of the brute. We can know God only by knowing ourselves, for our natures are similar to His. Man has been created in the image of God. If the methods here suggested are earnestly practised, you will know yourself to be a Blissful spirit and will realize God. In these things there is nothing that is found in Christianity and not also in Mahomedanism and Hinduism, not in the latter that is not in the former. Further, the methods laid down embrace all the conceivable means essential to the realization of God. They do leave out of consideration the thousand and one conventional rules and minor practices enjoined by the so-called different religions, because some of these relate to differences in the frame of mind of the individuals, hence are less important, though by no means unnecessary, and because others come up in the course of practice of these methods, hence do not require fuller treatment in our limited space.

The superiority of this method over others lies in the fact that it lays its hand just on the thing that binds us down to our narrow individuality—the *life-force* that, instead of being turned back and absorbed into the expansive self-conscious force of the self, goes outward, keeps our body and mind always in motion, and causes disturbances to the Spiritual self, in the shape of bodily sensations and passing thoughts. Because *life-force* moves outward, sensations and thoughts disturb and distort the calm image of "Self"-consciousness. This method teaches us to turn the life-force inward. Hence it is *direct* and *immediate*. It takes us straight to the consciousness of the "Self"—Bliss-God. It does not require the help of an intermediary. It controls and directs the course of the life-force by the control and regulation of a known and directly connected *manifestation* of the life-force itself. (It is not desirable nor is it possible that this process be explained further in this book.)

The other methods employ the help of the

intellect, or thought process, to control the *life-force* in order to induce consciousness of the "Self" in its Bliss-ful and other aspects. It should be noted that all religious methods in the world directly or indirectly, tacitly or expressly, enjoin the control, regulation, and turning back of the *life-force* so that we may transcend the body and mind and know the "Self" in its native state. The fourth method directly controls itself by itself, whereas the other methods do it through some other intermediary—thought, prayer, worship or meditation, etc.

Presence of life in man is existence, absence of it is death. Hence the method that teaches life's direct power to control itself must be the best of all.

Now savants of different ages and climes have suggested methods adapted to the mental frame and condition of the people among whom they lived and preached. Some have laid stress on prayer, some on feeling, some on love, some on reason or thought, some on meditation. But their motives have been the same.

They all meant that body should be transcended by the control and turning back of the *life-force* inward, and that the "Self" should be realized as the image of the sun in a calm, unruffled water. Their purpose is the inculcation of just that which the fourth method teaches directly, without the help of any intermediary.

At the same time it should be noted that the practice of this method does not prevent the cultivation of the intellect, the building up of the physique, and the activity of a social and useful life,—a life of the best feelings and motives, devoted to philanthropic works. As a matter of fact, *all-sided training* should be prescribed for all. It positively helps rather than retards the practice of the method; the only thing required is that its point of view be retained. Then all actions, all pursuits, will result to our advantage.

The main thing in this process, in a word, is to understand thoroughly the mystery of the life-force that sustains the bodily organism of man, causing it to vibrate with life and energy, illumine the intellect, and build up a strong physique, for the creation of the ideal social man. Unless we understand what we are and what the life with which we have daily connection means, our knowledge is imperfect. So I say we should analyze the life of man, as it were, in a laboratory, find out what it is, and then devise means to make it what it ought to be. This process is not of my own invention; it has been found to be universally true in all climes and ages. Truth is always found to be the same everywhere and by every one. Only, some times it is out of our sight. Though seeing, we see not, hearing, we hear not. I have only wished to relate what I have found through the help of others.

CHAPTER III

INSTRUMENTS OF KNOWLEDGE: RELIGIOUS POINT OF VIEW

The universality and necessity of the Religious Ideal (Ever-existent, Ever-conscious Bliss-God) and the practical methods to reach it have been discussed in the previous chapters. Now we wish to discuss the grounds of validity of the methods. The methods are essentially practical, and if they are followed the ideal must be reached, whether we deal with the theories or not. Their ground of validity is the practical result itself, which is palpable and real. It is not, be it understood, really necessary to show the theoretical grounds of validity. But simply to satisfy others we treat *a priori* of the validity of the theories of knowledge on which the methods are based, that their validity may also be theoretically shown. This will launch us into the epistemological question: How and how far can we know the Ideal, the Truth? To show how we know the ideal we must consider how we know the actual world. We must deal with the process of knowing the world. Then we shall see whether the process of knowing the world is the same as the process of knowing the Ideal, and whether the actual world is separate from the Ideal or whether the latter pervades the former, only the process of knowing the two being different. Before proceeding further let us discuss the "instruments" of knowledge—the way by which knowledge of the world is made possible to us.

There are three *instruments* or *means* of knowledge: *Perception, Inference, Intuition.*

I. PERCEPTION. Our senses are, as it were, windows, through which stimuli from the outside come and strike the mind, which passively receives these impressions. Unless the mind operates, no impression can be made on it by the stimuli coming from the outside through the sense-windows. Mind not only furnishes the connections to the stimuli received through the different senses, but stores their influences in the form of impressions. But these impressions remain a confused, disconnected mass until the discriminative faculty (Buddhi) operates on the impressions. A relevant connection is then established and the details of the outer world are recognized as such. They are projected, so to speak, and known in the forms of time and space, having distinct associations—quantity, quality, measure, and meaning. A house is then known as a house, and not as a post. This is the result of the operation of the Intellect (Buddhi). First we see an object, feel it, and then hear the sound of it when struck, our mind receiving these impressions and storing them. Buddhi interprets them and seems to project them in the form of a house with its various parts—size, shape, color, form, fashion, and its relation to others in the present, past, or future—in time and space. This is how knowledge of the world arises. An insane person has impressions stored in his mind, but they are in a chaotic state—not sorted and made up into distinct, well-ordered groups by Buddhi (Intellect).

Now comes the question: Can Reality (the Ideal, Ever-conscious, Ever-existent, Bliss-God) be known by perception of this sort? Is the process of knowing this world, viz., by perception, valid in the matter of knowing the Highest truth?

Now we know Buddhi can work only upon the materials supplied by the senses. It is certain that the senses give us only the stimuli of qualities and variety. Not only do the senses give variety, but Buddhi itself deals with variety and remains in the region of variety. Though it can think of "unity in diversity," it cannot be one with it. This is its drawback. Perception can not really give the true nature of Substance—One, Universal—underlying diverse manifestations. This is the verdict of Reason itself. When Buddhi (in the broad sense, thought) turns back upon itself to judge how far, by interpreting the sense-impressions, it is capable of knowing Reality, it finds itself hopelessly shut up within the domain of the sense-world. There is no loop-hole through which it can peep into the super-sensuous world.

Some may say that because we drive a wedge between the sensuous and the super-sensuous worlds, Reason can not bring itself to believe that it can have any knowledge of the super-sensuous. They say that if we think of the super-sensuous as manifesting in and through the sensuous, then in knowing the sensuous—with its connection (teleology, or adaptation) and all the details and varieties by the processes of the intellect—we shall be knowing the super-sensuous manifested as "unity in diversity." But it may be questioned, what is the nature of that *knowing?* Is it merely an idea in our brain, or is it *seeing* the truth (unity in diversity) face to face, first-hand and direct? Does that form of *knowing* carry the same conviction which being one with it would carry? Surely not, for that *knowing* is very partial, defective. It is merely looking through a colored glass. The super-sensuous world lies beyond. These are the *a priori* arguments against perception as an instrument for knowing Reality, or God.

From calm experience, also, we find that we can not attain that Blissful state, which is Reality and the Ideal itself, as shown in the previous chapters, until we rise to a considerable extent from the restless, perceptual stage. The more we leave behind the disturbing perceptions and interior thoughts, the greater is the possibility of the dawning of that supermental state of Bliss, or Bliss-God. Ordinary perception and Bliss seem to be mutually exclusive in common experience. However, none of our methods is based on pure perception, hence the inability of the latter to know Reality does not affect the former.

II. INFERENCE. This is another way of deriving knowledge of the world. But inference itself is based on experience,—on perception,—be it deductive or inductive. In our experience we find fire wherever there is smoke; hence if we see smoke on any occasion, we infer there is fire. This is deductive inference. But it is possible only because of our previous experience (perception) of smoke as being associated with fire. In inductive inference, also, there is the same dependence on perception. We observe that a certain kind of bacillus is the cause of cholera. We find out the causal connection between that kind of bacillus and cholera and at once inductively infer that wherever we find this bacillus, cholera will be present. While there is a leap here from the known cases of cholera to the unknown cases, still by inference we get no new fact, though the cases may be new. The very possibility of the establishment of causal connection between bacilli and cholera depended upon observation (perception) of certain cases. So inference ultimately depends upon perception. In inferred cases we do not get any new truth—nothing really new that was not found in observed cases. In observed cases bacilli are followed by cholera, and in the inferred cases, too, bacilli are followed by cholera—no new truth, though the cases are fresh and new.

So in all forms of thought, reasoning, inference, or imagination we are not face to face with Reality. Reason or thought may arrange and systematize facts of experience. It can endeavor to see things as a whole. It may try to penetrate into the mystery of the world. But its effort is hampered by the materials on which it works—facts of experience, sense impressions. They are bald, hard facts, disconnected, limited by our powers of perception. The materials disturb rather than help the thought process, which also has a restless continuity.

The first method, as we pointed out, is the intellectual method. It busies itself with the thought process in order to know Reality—state of Bliss and calm realization. But it fails. Bodily perceptions disturb, and the thought process also, due to its working on varied, restless sense-impressions, forbids our remaining for long in a concentrated state, that we may know and feel that calm condition of Bliss and have the consciousness of unity in diversity. One merit of the Intellectual method is that when we are absorbed in the thought-world, to a certain extent we transcend bodily sensations. But this is always temporary.

In the other two methods—Devotional and Meditation—the thought process is less. Still, it is present. In the devotional method, i.e., in ritual worship or otherwise, in prayer, congregational or individual, much of the thought-process is engaged in the arrangement of favorable conditions. Still there is the attempt to concentrate on some subject of worship or prayer. So far as the diversity in thought processes is checked or prevented, the devotional method is successful. Still the defect is this: due to our bad habit, confirmed in the course of ages, our concentration is not deep, leaving the possibility of setting the diversity of thought-processes at work on the slightest disturbance.

In the Meditation method outward formalities, conventions, rites, etc., being dispensed with, thus barring the possibility of the thought-processes being set into motion as easily as in the Devotional method, concentration is fixed on one object of thought. And there is a gradual tendency to leave the sphere of thought to step into that of Intuition, which we shall next consider.

III. INTUITION. So far we have been considering the instruments and processes of knowing this sensuous world. Intuition, with which we now deal, is the process by which we know the super-sensuous world—the world that is beyond senses and thoughts. It is true that the super-sensuous expresses itself in and through the sensuous, and to know the latter in completeness is to know the former, but the process of knowing the two must be different. To know the latter, perception and thought will be fairly sufficient, but to know the super-sensuous, Intuition is required. It is no argument to say that because the super-sensuous expresses itself through the sensuous, the process of knowing the latter (Perception and Thought) will also hold good in the case of the former. For, are we able to know the *sensuous world even*, in all its fullness, by these processes? Assuredly not. There is an infinite number of facts, things, laws, connections in nature, and even in our own organism, which are still and probably ever will be a sealed book to mankind. Far less, then, shall we be able to know what is really beyond sense-perception and thought-perception by mere sense and thought.

Intuition comes from within; thought from without. The former gives a face-to-face view of Reality; the latter gives an indirect view of it. Intuition, by a strange sympathy, sees it in its totality, while thought chops it up into parts. Every man has the power of intuition, as he has the power of thought. As thought can be cultivated, so Intuition can be developed. In Intuition we are in tune with Reality—with the world of Bliss, with the "unity in diversity" with the inner laws governing the spiritual world, with God.

How do we know that we exist? Through sense-perception? Do the senses first tell us that we *exist*—whence the consciousness of existence comes? That can never be. For the consciousness of existence is pre-supposed in the attempt of the senses to let us know of *our* existence. Sense cannot consciously sense anything without our first knowing that *we exist* in the very act of sensing. Does inference, the thought-process, tell us that *we* exist? Assuredly not. For the materials of thought must be sense-impressions, which, as we have just found, cannot tell us of our existence, as that feeling is already pre-supposed in them. Nor can the process of thought give us the consciousness of existence, for the latter is already implied in the former. When, by comparing ourselves with the outer world, we endeavor to think or infer that *we exist* therein, the consciousness of existence is already present in the very act of thinking and inferring. Then, if sense or thought fails, how do we know that *we exist?* It is only by Intuition that we can know this. This knowing is *one form* of Intuition. It is beyond sense and thought—they are made possible by it.

It is very difficult to define Intuition, for it is too near to every one of us. Every one of us feels it. Do we not know what the consciousness of existence is? Every one knows it. It is too familiar to admit of definition. Ask one how he knows *he exists.* He will remain dumb. He knows it, but he cannot define it. He may try to explain, but his explanation does not reveal what he inwardly feels. *Intuition of every form has this peculiar character.*

The fourth method, explained in the last chapter, bases itself on Intuition. The practice of it leads us inward. The more earnest we are about it, the wider and surer will be our vision of Reality—God. It is through Intuition that humanity reaches Divinity, that the sensuous is brought into connection with the super-sensuous, and that the latter is *felt* to express itself in and through the sensuous. The influence of senses vanishes, intruding thoughts disappear, Bliss-God is realized, the consciousness of "all in One and One in all" dawns upon us. This Intuition is what all great savants and prophets of the world had and still have.

The third method (Meditation-Method), as explained in the last chapter, when it is earnestly practised, carries us also into the region of Intuition. But it is a bit roundabout, and ordinarily takes a longer time to produce in us the successive states of the Intuitional or Realization process.

Thus it is by Intuition that God can be realized in *all His aspects*. We have no sense that can reveal knowledge of Him. The senses give knowledge of only His manifestations. No thought or inference can enable us to know Him as He truly is. For thought cannot go beyond what the senses give. It can only arrange and interpret the impressions of the senses. When the senses are unable, thought, as depending upon them, is also unable to bring us to God. So it is to Intuition that we shall have to turn for the knowledge of God in His Blissful and other aspects.

Religion is truly an act of Intuition; without it the former degrades into the observance of lifeless conventions and rites. It is from the point of view of Intuition that every fact of the world finds meaning in its totality. The criterion of development in the Spiritual world is also Intuition. Men of the world will see how far you are punctual, regular, and devoted in the matter of observing the codes and canons of worldly-wise morality and Religion, but the seer of truth will mark how far you have progressed in the path of realization—Intuition.

But there are many bars to this Religious point of view—to the realization of truth. These are some of them: Disease, Mental Incapacity, Doubt, Indolence, Worldly-mindedness, False Notion, Missing the Point and Instability.

These are either inherent or engendered and

aggravated through association with others. Besides the above there may be many other inherent tendencies (*Samskaras*) which turn out to be the causes of these. We seem to have no control over our *Samskaras*, but our strong-minded effort (*Purushakara*) can work wonders. It can change them, nay, it can destroy them. When they are changed for the better they help rather than retard us. It is through effort, as facilitated by association with the good, that new tendencies (*Samskaras*) can be formed and the bad ones changed.

Until we associate with those who have seen, felt, and realized Religion in their lives we can not fully know what it is, and in what its universality and necessity lie.

Everybody in the world is a seeker after truth. The spirit of inquiry is in all. But it is dulled and the willingness to know the truth is dampened, because distractions are many, tendencies are or grow to be perverse, and monsters of the world are also numerous.

But still we are men, not animals. It is never too late to mend or seek. Search and you will find, "Knock, and it shall be opened unto you."

OM